THE FLOWERS I LOVE

THE FLOWERS I LOVE

A SERIES OF TWENTY-FOUR DRAWINGS IN COLOUR BY

KATHARINE CAMERON

WITH AN ANTHOLOGY OF FLOWER POEMS

SELECTED BY

EDWARD THOMAS

Edward Thomas

Philip Edward Thomas was born in Lambeth, London, England in 1878. His parents were Welsh migrants, and Thomas attended several schools, before ending up at St. Pauls. Never entirely happy with urban life – he took many trips to Wiltshire and Wales, fostering an attraction to the natural world which would inform much of his later poetry – Thomas led a reclusive early life, and began writing as a teenager. He published his first book, *The Woodland Life* (1897), at the age of just nineteen. A year later, he won a history scholarship to Lincoln College, Oxford.

In 1899, while still an undergraduate, Thomas married Helen Noble, daughter of the essayist and poet James Ashcroft Noble (1844-1896). Encouraged by his wife's father, Thomas committed himself to becoming a man of letters. He worked frantically, reviewing up to fifteen books a week (usually poetry collections) for the *Daily Chronicle*, and penning six collections of essays in eight years. Thomas was a skilful critic; in 1913, *The Times* described him as "the man with the keys to the Paradise of English poetry." He also became a close friend of the Welsh poet W. H. Davies, whose career he almost single-handedly developed.

Thomas was never entirely happy with life as a prolific essayist, however. In correspondence with the poet Gordon Bottomely, he described himself as a hack writer, a "hurried and harried prose man" whose exhaustion left his brain "wild." Thomas suffered from chronic depression, apparently carrying a vial of poison (which he described as his "saviour") with him at all times. In 1911, he suffered a severe mental breakdown.

In the spring of 1914, in what was arguably the most formative event of his life, Thomas met the American poet Robert Frost. Although Frost is now one of America's most adored poets, at this point no one would publish his work in the United States, and he had emigrated to England in search of artistic fortune. Thomas had previously reviewed Frost's work at great length, and, upon meeting, the men engaged in lengthly discussions on the nature and form of poetry.

On one of their many long countryside walks, Frost suggested to Thomas that sections of his *In Pursuit of Spring* (1913) – a meditative travelogue documenting Thomas' pilgrimage by bicycle from Clapham Common, London, to the Quantock Hills of Somerset – might be turned into poems. Together, the two men experimented with composing lines that followed, in loose poetic form, the sound-patterns of speech – building on theories of rhythm and form Thomas had expressed in his critiques of *Algernon Charles Swinburne* (1912) and *Walter Pater* (1913).

Frost's advice turned out to be transformative. Thomas returned to his accumulated writings with new imagination. He began to pen loose and lyrical poems, calling them "quintessences of the best parts of my prose books" which purged the stultifying effects of "damned rhetoric" from his writing. As well as being a creative release, Thomas found the process of writing poetry to be highly therapeutic; in his journals, he spoke of them as fostering a sense of strong mental calm.

Thomas began writing poetry seriously in December of 1914 – five months after the onset of World War I. He published several poems under the pseudonym Edward Eastaway, which variously baffled and delighted reviewers. Meanwhile, he deliberated over whether to join the war effort or not (Frost penned what would become his most famous poem, "The Road Not Taken", in response to Thomas's dilemma).

Eventually, despite being overage, Thomas enlisted in a voluntary unit in July 1915. He then returned to his poetry with a renewed vigour. However, Thomas was not a war poet in the same sense as Wilfred Owen or Siegfried Sassoon – the trenches barely feature in his work, and he only wrote one poem after reaching France – nor was he any less conflicted than these men about the conflict. For Thomas, World War I compounded a range of complex feelings he harboured regarding England, the countryside, culture and identity. Speaking of his enlistment in the essay 'This Is England', he said "Something, I felt, had to be done before I could again look composedly at English landscape." However, he stressed elsewhere that "I hate not Germans nor grow hot/ With love of Englishmen, to please newspapers."

In November 1916, Thomas was commissioned into the Royal Garrison Artillery as a second lieutenant. Soon after arriving in France, Thomas was involved in the Battle of Arras, a British offensive. On Easter Monday (9th April), while standing to light his pipe, one of the last shells fired during the battle landed close to him, causing a concussive blast from which he didn't recover. He was aged 39.

Despite being less well-known than other World War I poets, Thomas is regarded by many critics as one of the finest. Since the seventies, five new anthologies of his verse have appeared (the vast majority of Thomas' work wasn't published during his brief literary life), and the longtime British Poet Laureate Ted Hughes went so far as to call him the "father of us all." In 2011, a biography of Thomas by Matthew Hollis entitled *Now All Roads Lead to France: The Last Years of Edward Thomas* won the Costa Biography Award.

In 1985, Thomas was among sixteen World War I poets commemorated on a slate stone unveiled in Westminster Abbey's Poet's Corner. Meanwhile, in Steep, East Hampshire – where Thomas and his wife lived between 1913 and 1916, and where he composed the bulk of his poems – a memorial stone has been erected to the memory of the poet. The stone's inscription includes the final line from his essay collection, *Light and Twilight* (1911): "And I rose up and knew I was tired and I continued my journey."

ACKNOWLEDGMENTS

PERMISSION has been kindly given to use copyright poems from the following volumes :

Gordon Bottomley : *The Gate of Smaragdus*, and *Chambers of Imagery* (Elkin Mathews).

Robert Bridges : *Poetical Works* (Smith Elder).

Charles Dalmon : *Song Favours* (John Lane), and *Flower and Leaf* (Grant Richards).

William H. Davies : *New Poems* (Elkin Mathews), *Farewell to Poesy* (A. C. Fifield), and *Nature Poems* (Fifield).

Walter de la Mare : *Songs of Childhood* (Longmans), *Poems* (Murray), *The Listeners* (Constable), and *Peacock Pie* (Constable).

Vivian Locke Ellis : *The Venturers* (21 York Buildings, Adelphi).

Robert Frost : *A Boy's Will* (David Nutt).

Ralph Hodgson : *Eve and other Poems* (Poetry Bookshop, 35 Devonshire Street, Theobald's Road, London, W.C.).

D. H. Lawrence : *Georgian Poetry* (Poetry Bookshop).

Rose Macaulay : *The Two Blind Countries* (Sidgwick and Jackson).

Henry Newbolt : *Poems New and Old* (Murray).

Francis Thompson : *Collected Works* (Burns and Oates).

CONTENTS

viii

LIST OF PLATES

HARK ! HARK !

HARK ! hark ! the lark at heaven's gate sings,
  And Phœbus 'gins arise,
His steeds to water at those springs
  On chaliced flowers that lies ;
And winking Mary-buds begin
  To ope their golden eyes ;
With every thing that pretty is,
  My lady sweet, arise ;
    Arise, arise.

SHAKESPEARE

SONGS FROM 'ARCADES'

I

O'ER the smooth enamelled green,
  Where no print of step hath been,
    Follow me, as I sing
    And touch the warbled string :
Under the shady roof
Of branching elm star-proof
    Follow me.
I will bring you where she sits,
Clad in splendour as befits
    Her deity.
Such a rural Queen
All Arcadia hath not seen.

A

I

II

Nymphs and Shepherds, dance no more
  By sandy Ladon's lilied banks ;
On old Lycæus, or Cyllene hoar,
  Trip no more in twilight ranks ;
Though Erymanth your loss deplore,
  A better soil shall give ye thanks.
From the stony Mænalus
Bring your flocks, and live with us ;
Here ye shall have greater grace,
To serve the Lady of this place.
Though Syrinx your Pan's mistress were,
Yet Syrinx well might wait on her.
  Such a rural Queen
  All Arcadia hath not seen.

MILTON

TO MEADOWS

YE have been fresh and green,
  Ye have been fill'd with flowers ;
And ye the walks have been
  Where maids have spent their hours.

You have beheld how they
  With wicker arks did come
To kiss and bear away
  The richer cowslips home.

Ye 've heard them sweetly sing,
  And seen them in a round ;
Each virgin, like a spring,
  With honeysuckles crowned.

But now, we see none here,
   Whose silvery feet did tread,
And with dishevelled hair
   Adorned this smoother mead.

Like unthrifts, having spent
   Your stock, and needy grown,
Ye 're left here to lament
   Your poor estates, alone.

HERRICK

COME INTO THE GARDEN, MAUD

COME into the garden, Maud,
   For the black bat, night, has flown,
Come into the garden, Maud,
   I am here at the gate alone ;
And the woodbine spices are wafted abroad,
   And the musk of the rose is blown.

For a breeze of morning moves,
   And the planet of Love is on high,
Beginning to faint in the light that she loves
   On a bed of daffodil sky,
To faint in the light of the sun she loves,
   To faint in his light, and to die.

All night have the roses heard
   The flute, violin, bassoon ;
All night has the casement jessamine stirr'd
   To the dancers dancing in tune ;
Till a silence fell with the waking bird,
   And a hush with the setting moon.

3

I said to the lily, ' There is but one
    With whom she has heart to be gay.
When will the dancers leave her alone ?
    She is weary of dance and play.'
Now half to the setting moon are gone,
    And half to the rising day ;
Low on the sand and loud on the stone
    The last wheel echoes away.

I said to the rose, ' The brief night goes
    In babble and revel and wine.
O young lord-lover, what sighs are those,
    For one that will never be thine ?
But mine, but mine,' so I sware to the rose,
    ' For ever and ever, mine.'

And the soul of the rose went into my blood,
    As the music clash'd in the hall ;
And long by the garden lake I stood,
    For I heard your rivulet fall
From the lake to the meadow and on to the wood,
    Our wood, that is dearer than all ;

From the meadow your walks have left so sweet
    That whenever a March-wind sighs
He sets the jewel-print of your feet
    In violets blue as your eyes,
To the woody hollows in which we meet
    And the valleys of Paradise.

The slender acacia would not shake
    One long milk-bloom on the tree ;
The white lake-blossom fell into the lake
    As the pimpernel dozed on the lea ;

4

DREAM ROSES

But the rose was awake all night for your sake,
    Knowing your promise to me ;
The lilies and roses were all awake,
    They sigh'd for the dawn and thee.

There has fallen a splendid tear
    From the passion-flower at the gate.
She is coming, my dove, my dear ;
    She is coming, my life, my fate ;
The red rose cries, ' She is near, she is near ' ;
    And the white rose weeps, ' She is late ' ;
The larkspur listens, ' I hear, I hear ' ;
    And the lily whispers, ' I wait.'

She is coming, my own, my sweet ;
    Were it ever so airy a tread,
My heart would hear her and beat,
    Were it earth in an earthy bed ;
My dust would hear her and beat,
    Had I lain for a century dead ;
Would start and tremble under her feet,
    And blossom in purple and red.

TENNYSON

THE THREE CHERRY TREES

THERE were three cherry trees once,
    Grew in a garden all shady ;
And there for delight of so gladsome a sight,
    Walked a most beautiful lady,
    Dreamed a most beautiful lady.

5

Birds in those branches did sing,
Blackbird and throstle and linnet,
But she walking there was by far the most fair—
Lovelier than all else within it,
Blackbird and throstle and linnet.

But blossoms to berries do come,
All hanging on stalks light and slender,
And one long summer's day charmed that lady away,
With vows sweet and merry and tender ;
A lover with voice low and tender.

Moss and lichen the green branches deck ;
Weeds nod in its paths green and shady :
Yet a light footstep seems to wander in dreams,
The ghost of that beautiful lady,
That happy and beautiful lady.

WALTER DE LA MARE

MOWING

THERE was never a sound beside the wood but one,
And that was my long scythe whispering to the ground.
What was it it whispered ?   I knew not well myself ;
Perhaps it was something about the heat of the sun,
Something, perhaps, about the lack of sound—
And that was why it whispered and did not speak.
It was no dream of the gift of idle hours,
Or easy gold at the hand of fay or elf :
Anything more than the truth would have seemed too
        weak
To the earnest love that laid the swale in rows,
Not without feeble-pointed spikes of flowers

6

NOVEMBER

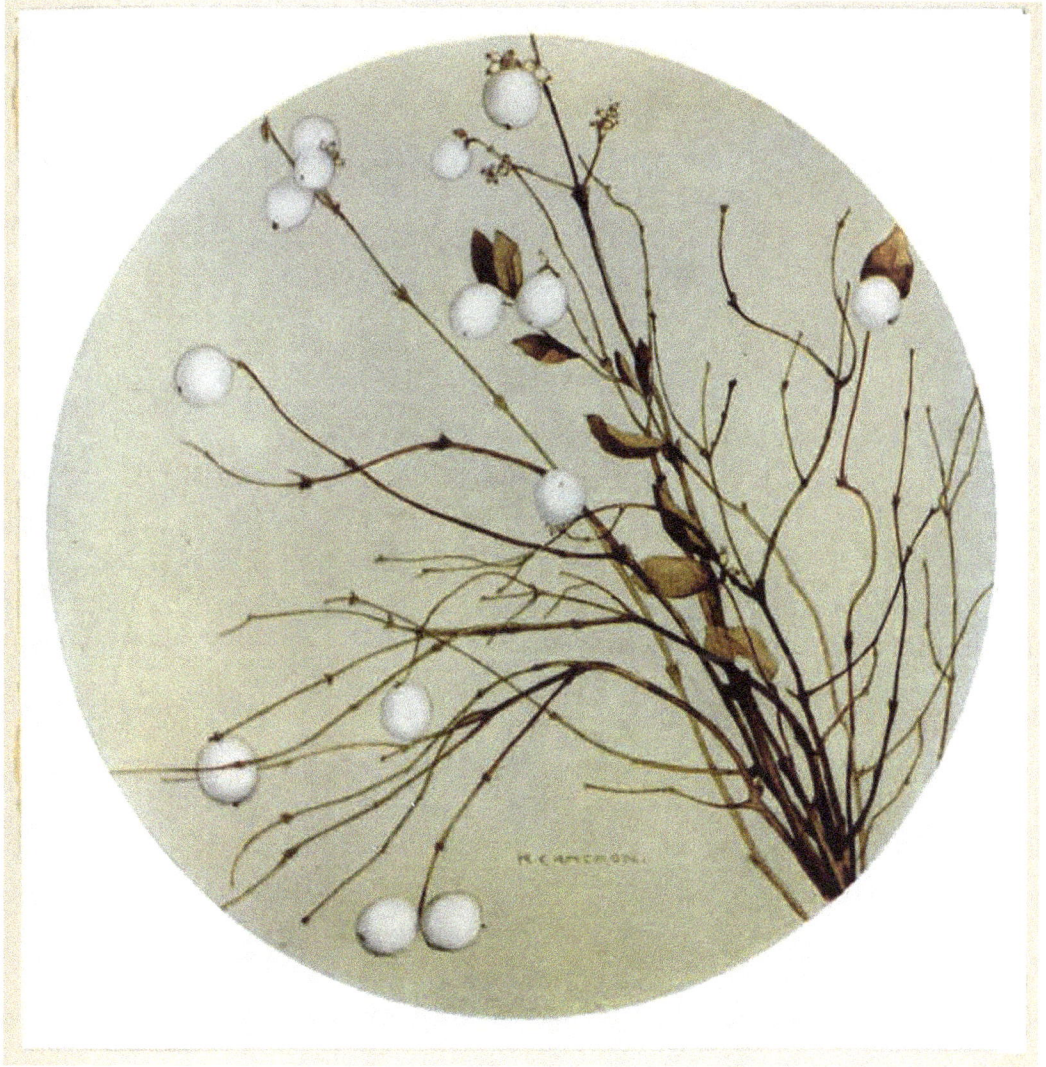

(Pale orchises), and scared a bright green snake.
The fact is the sweetest dream that labour knows.
My long scythe whispered and left the hay to make.

ROBERT FROST

TO A NIGHTINGALE

MY heart aches, and a drowsy numbness pains
   My sense, as though of hemlock I had drunk,
Or emptied some dull opiate to the drains
   One minute past, and Lethe-wards had sunk :
'Tis not through envy of thy happy lot,
   But being too happy in thy happiness,—
      That thou, light-winged Dryad of the trees,
        In some melodious plot
   Of beechen green, and shadows numberless,
   Singest of summer in full-throated ease.

O for a draught of vintage, that hath been
   Cool'd a long age in the deep-delved earth,
Tasting of Flora and the country green,
   Dance, and Provençal song, and sun-burnt mirth !
O for a beaker full of the warm South,
   Full of the true, the blushful Hippocrene,
      With beaded bubbles winking at the brim,
        And purple-stained mouth ;
   That I might drink, and leave the world unseen,
   And with thee fade away into the forest dim.

Fade far away, dissolve, and quite forget
   What thou among the leaves hast never known,
The weariness, the fever, and the fret
   Here, where men sit and hear each other groan ;

7

Where palsy shakes a few, sad, last grey hairs,
  Where youth grows pale, and spectre-thin, and dies;
    Where but to think is to be full of sorrow
      And leaden-eyed despairs;
  Where Beauty cannot keep her lustrous eyes,
    Or new Love pine at them beyond to-morrow.

Away! away! for I will fly to thee,
  Not charioted by Bacchus and his pards,
But on the viewless wings of Poesy,
  Though the dull brain perplexes and retards:
Already with thee! tender is the night,
  And haply the Queen-Moon is on her throne,
    Cluster'd around by all her starry Fays;
      But here there is no light,
  Save what from heaven is with the breezes blown
    Through verdurous glooms and winding mossy
      ways.

I cannot see what flowers are at my feet,
  Nor what soft incense hangs upon the boughs,
But, in embalmed darkness, guess each sweet
  Wherewith the seasonable month endows
The grass, the thicket, and the fruit-tree wild;
  White hawthorn and the pastoral eglantine;
    Fast-fading violets cover'd up in leaves;
      And mid-May's eldest child,
  The coming musk-rose, full of dewy wine,
    The murmurous haunt of flies on summer eves.

Darkling I listen; and for many a time
  I have been half in love with easeful Death,
Call'd him soft names in many a mused rhyme,
  To take into the air my quiet breath;
8

Now more than ever seems it rich to die,
　To cease upon the midnight with no pain,
　　While thou art pouring forth thy soul abroad
　　　In such an ecstasy !
　Still wouldst thou sing, and I have ears in vain—
　　To thy high requiem become a sod.

Thou wast not born for death, immortal Bird !
　No hungry generations tread thee down ;
The voice I hear this passing night was heard
　In ancient days by emperor and clown :
Perhaps the self-same song that found a path
　Through the sad heart of Ruth, when, sick for home,
　　She stood in tears amid the alien corn ;
　　　The same that ofttimes hath
Charm'd magic casements, opening on the foam
　Of perilous seas, in faery lands forlorn.

Forlorn ! the very word is like a bell
　To toll me back from thee to my sole self.
Adieu ! the fancy cannot cheat so well
　As she is famed to do, deceiving elf.
Adieu ! adieu ! thy plaintive anthem fades
　Past the near meadows, over the still stream,
　　Up the hill-side ; and now 'tis buried deep
　　　In the next valley-glades :
　Was it a vision, or a waking dream ?
　　Fled is that music :—do I wake or sleep ?

KEATS.

B　　　　　　　　　　　　　　　　　　　　9

THIS LIME-TREE BOWER

WELL, they are gone, and here must I remain,
This lime-tree bower my prison! I have lost
Beauties and feelings, such as would have been
Most sweet to my remembrance even when age
Had dimmed my eyes to blindness! They, mean-
    while,
Friends, whom I never more may meet again,
On springy heath, along the hill-top edge,
Wander in gladness, and wind down, perchance,
To that still roaring dell, of which I told ;
The roaring dell, o'erwooded, narrow, deep,
And only speckled by the mid-day sun ;
Where its slim trunk the ash from rock to rock
Flings arching like a bridge ;—that branchless ash,
Unsunned and damp, whose few poor yellow leaves
Ne'er tremble to the gale, yet tremble still,
Fanned by the waterfall! and there my friends
Behold the dark green file of long lank weeds,
That all at once (a most fantastic sight !)
Still nod and drip beneath the dripping edge
Of the blue clay-stone.
                            Now, my friends emerge
Beneath the wide wide heaven—and view again
The many-steepled tract magnificent
Of hilly fields and meadows, and the sea,
With some fair bark, perhaps, whose sails light up
The slip of smooth clear blue betwixt two isles
Of purple shadow ! Yes ! they wander on
In gladness all ; but thou, methinks, most glad,
My gentle-hearted Charles ! for thou hast pined
And hungered after Nature, many a year,
In the great city pent, winning thy way

10

With sad yet patient soul, through evil and pain
And strange calamity ! Ah ! slowly sink
Behind the western ridge, thou glorious sun !
Shine in the slant beams of the sinking orb,
Ye purple heath-flowers ! richlier burn, ye clouds !
Live in the yellow light, ye distant groves !
And kindle, thou blue ocean ! So my friend
Struck with deep joy may stand, as I have stood,
Silent with swimming sense ; yea, gazing round
On the wide landscape, gaze till all doth seem
Less gross than bodily ; and of such hues
As veil the Almighty Spirit, when yet He makes
Spirits perceive His presence.
       A delight
Comes sudden on my heart, and I am glad
As I myself were there ! Nor in this bower,
This little lime-tree bower, have I not marked
Much that has soothed me. Pale beneath the blaze
Hung the transparent foliage ; and I watched
Some broad and sunny leaf, and loved to see
The shadow of the leaf and stem above
Dappling its sunshine ! And that walnut-tree
Was richly tinged, and a deep radiance lay
Full on the ancient ivy, which usurps
Those fronting elms, and now, with blackest mass
Makes their dark branches gleam a lighter hue
Through the late twilight : and though now the bat
Wheels silent by, and not a swallow twitters,
Yet still the solitary humble-bee
Sings in the bean-flower ! Henceforth I shall know
That Nature ne'er deserts the wise and pure,
No plot so narrow, be but Nature there,
No waste so vacant, but may well employ
Each faculty of sense, and keep the heart

Awake to love and beauty ! and sometimes
'Tis well to be bereft of promised good,
That we may lift the soul, and contemplate·
With lively joy the joys we cannot share.
My gentle-hearted Charles ! when the last rook
Beat its straight path along the dusky air
Homeward, I blest it ! deeming its black wing
(Now a dim speck, now vanishing in light)
Had cross'd the mighty orb's dilated glory,
While thou stoodst gazing ; or when all was still,
Flew creaking o'er thy head, and had a charm
For thee, my gentle-hearted Charles, to whom
No sound is dissonant which tells of life.

COLERIDGE.

THE QUESTION

I DREAMED that, as I wandered by the way,
  Bare winter suddenly was changed to spring,
And gentle odours led my steps astray,
  Mixed with a sound of waters murmuring
Along a shelving bank of turf, which lay
  Under a copse, and hardly dared to fling
Its green arms round the bosom of the stream,
But kissed it and then fled, as thou mightest in dream.

There grew pied wind-flowers and violets,
  Daisies, those pearled Arcturi of the earth,
The constellated flower that never sets ;
  Faint oxlips ; tender bluebells, at whose birth
The sod scarce heaved; and that tall flower that wets—
  Like a child, half in tenderness and mirth—
Its mother's face with heaven's collected tears,
When the low wind, its playmate's voice, it hears.

12

And in the warm hedge grew lush eglantine,
　　Green cowbind and the moonlight-coloured may,
And cherry-blossoms, and white cups, whose wine
　　Was the bright dew, yet drained not by the day ;
And wild roses, and ivy serpentine,
　　With its dark buds and leaves, wandering astray ;
And flowers azure, black, and streaked with gold,
Fairer than any wakened eyes behold.

And nearer to the river's trembling edge
　　There grew broad flag-flowers, purple prankt with
　　　　white,
And starry river-buds among the sedge,
　　And floating water-lilies, broad and bright,
Which lit the oak that overhung the hedge
　　With moonlight beams of their own watery light ;
And bulrushes, and reeds of such deep green
As soothed the dazzled eye with sober sheen.

Methought that of these visionary flowers
　　I made a nosegay, bound in such a way
That the same hues, which in their natural bowers
　　Were mingled or opposed, the like array
Kept these imprisoned children of the Hours
　　Within my hand,—and then, elate and gay,
I hastened to the spot whence I had come,
That I might there present it !—oh, to whom ?
SHELLEY.

EVELYN HOPE

BEAUTIFUL Evelyn Hope is dead!
　　Sit and watch by her side an hour.
This is her book-shelf, this her bed;
　　She plucked that piece of geranium-flower,
Beginning to die too, in the glass;
　　Little has yet been changed, I think:
The shutters are shut, no light may pass
　　Save two long rays thro' the hinge's chink.

Sixteen years old when she died!
　　Perhaps she had scarcely heard my name;
It was not her time to love; beside,
　　Her life had many a hope and aim,
Duties enough and little cares,
　　And now was quiet, now astir,
Till God's hand beckoned unawares,—
　　And the sweet white brow is all of her.

Is it too late, then, Evelyn Hope?
　　What, your soul was pure and true,
The good stars met in your horoscope,
　　Made you of spirit, fire and dew—
And, just because I was thrice as old
　　And our paths in the world diverged so wide,
Each was nought to each, must I be told?
　　We were fellow mortals, nought beside?

No, indeed! for God above
　　Is great to grant, as mighty to make,
And created the love to reward the love:
　　I claim you still, for my own love's sake!
14

SCYLLAS

Delayed it may be for more lives yet,
  Through worlds I shall traverse, not a few :
Much is to learn, much to forget
  Ere the time be come for taking you.

But the time will come,—at last it will,
  When, Evelyn Hope, what meant (I shall say)
In the lower earth, in the years long still,
  That body and soul so pure and gay ?
Why your hair was amber, I shall divine,
  And your mouth of your own geranium's red—
And what you would do with me, in fine,
  In the new life come in the old one's stead.

I have lived (I shall say) so much since then,
  Given up myself so many times,
Gained me the gains of various men,
  Ransacked the ages, spoiled the climes ;
Yet one thing, one, in my soul's full scope,
  Either I missed or itself missed me :
And I want and find you, Evelyn Hope !
  What is the issue ? let us see !

I loved you, Evelyn, all the while,
  My heart seemed full as it could hold.
There was place and to spare for the frank young smile,
  And the red young mouth, and the hair's young gold.
So, hush,—I will give you this leaf to keep :
  See, I shut it inside the sweet cold hand !
There, that is our secret : go to sleep !
  You will wake, and remember, and understand.

BROWNING.

TO MISTRESS ISABEL PENNELL

BY Saint Mary, my lady,
Your mammy and your daddy
Brought forth a goodly baby.

My maiden Isabel,
Reflaring rosabel,
The flagrant camomel,

The ruddy rosary,
The sovereign rosemary,
The pretty strawberry,

The columbine, the nepte,
The gillyflower well set,
The proper violet,

Ennewèd your colour
Is like the daisy flower
After the April shower.

Star of the morrow gray,
The blossom on the spray,
The freshest flower of May,

Maidenly demure,
Of womanhood the lure ;
Wherefore I make you sure.

It were an heavenly health,
It were an endless wealth,
A life for God himself,

CAMOMILE

To hear this nightingale
Among the birdès small
Warbling in the vale,

'Dug, dug, jug, jug!
Good year and good luck!'
With 'Chuck, chuck, chuck, chuck!'

SKELTON.

O GIN MY LOVE

O WERE my love yon lilac fair,
  Wi' purple blossoms to the spring,
And I a bird to shelter there,
  When wearied on my little wing.

How I wad mourn when it was torn,
  By autumn wild, and winter rude!
But I wad sing on wanton wing,
  When youthfu' May its bloom renew'd.

O gin my love were yon red rose,
  That grows upon the castle wa',
And I mysel' a drap o' dew
  Into her bonnie breast to fa'!

O! there beyond expression blest,
  I'd feast on beauty a' the night;
Seal'd on her silk-saft faulds to rest,
  Till fley'd awa' by Phœbus' light.

BURNS.

C

BRIDAL SONG

ROSES, their sharp spines being gone,
Not royal in their smells alone,
    But in their hue ;
Maiden pinks, of odour faint,
Daisies smell-less, yet most quaint,
    And sweet thyme true ;

Primrose, firstborn child of Ver,
Merry springtime's harbinger,
    With harebells dim ;
Oxlips in their cradles growing,
Marigolds on deathbeds blowing,
    Larks'-heels trim.

All dear Nature's children sweet,
Lie 'fore bride and bridegroom's feet,
    Blessing their sense !
Not an angel of the air,
Bird melodious, or bird fair,
    Be absent hence !

The crow, the slanderous cuckoo, nor
The boding raven, nor chough hoar,
    Nor chattering pie,
May on our bride-house perch or sing,
Or with them any discord bring,
    But from it fly !
        FROM ' THE TWO NOBLE KINSMEN.'

GO, NOR ACQUAINT THE ROSE

GO, nor acquaint the Rose,
Nor Beauty's household, with that grief of thine.
Stand not in wait with those
Who with their knocking trouble the divine.

But thou, let Beauty be ;
Dread distance of her trancèd languors keep ;
If then she follow thee
When thou art treading noiseless from her sleep,

Rose then and wafted Rose,
Like summer past and summer's breath still there,
Shall render all she owes,
More than she ever yielded to thy prayer.

VIVIAN LOCKE ELLIS.

MALVOLIO

THOU hast been very tender to the moon,
Malvolio ! and on many a daffodil
And many a daisy hast thou yearn'd, until
The nether jaw quiver'd with thy good heart.
But tell me now, Malvolio, tell me true,
Hast thou not sometimes driven from their play
The village children, when they came too near
Thy study, if hit ball rais'd shouts around,
Or if delusive trap shook off thy muse,
Pregnant with wonders for another age ?
Hast thou sat still and patient (tho' sore prest
Hearthward to stoop and warm thy blue-nail'd hand)
Lest thou shouldst frighten from a frosty fare

19

The speckled thrush, raising his bill aloft
To swallow the red berry on the ash
By thy white window, three short paces off ?
If *this* thou hast not done, and hast done *that*,
I do exile thee from the moon twelve whole
Calendar months, debarring thee from use
Of rose, bud, blossom, odour, simile,
And furthermore I do hereby pronounce
Divorce between the nightingale and thee.

LANDOR.

SONNET

NYMPH of the garden where all beauties be,—
Beauties which do in excellency pass
His who till death looked in a watery glass,
Or hers whom naked the Troian boy did seé ;
Sweet garden-nymph, which keeps the cherry tree
Whose fruit does far the Hesperian taste surpass,
Most sweet-fair, most fair-sweet, do not, alas,
From coming near those cherries banish me.
For though, full of desire, empty of wit,
Admitted late by your best-graced grace,
I caught at one of them, and hungry bit ;
Pardon that fault ; once more grant me the place ;
And I do swear, even by the same delight,
I will but kiss ; I never more will bite.

SIDNEY.

ROSES IN A SATSUMA BOWL

NOW SLEEPS THE CRIMSON PETAL

NOW sleeps the crimson petal, now the white ;
Nor waves the cypress in the palace walk ;
Nor winks the gold fin in the porphyry font :
The fire-fly wakens : waken thou with me.

Now droops the milk-white peacock like a ghost,
And like a ghost she glimmers on to me.

Now lies the earth all Danaë to the stars,
And all thy heart lies open unto me.

Now slides the silent meteor on, and leaves
A shining furrow as thy thoughts in me.

Now folds the lily all her sweetness up,
And slips into the bosom of the lake :
So fold thyself, my dearest, thou, and slip
Into my bosom and be lost in me.

TENNYSON.

COMING TO KISS HER LIPS

COMING to kiss her lips (such grace I found),
Meseemed, I smelt a garden of sweet flowers,
That dainty odours from them threw around,
For damsels fit to deck their lovers' bowers.
Her lips did smell like unto Gillyflowers ;
Her ruddy cheeks, like unto Roses red ;
Her snowy brows, like budded Bellamours ;
Her lovely eyes, like Pinks but newly spread ;

21

Her goodly bosom, like a Strawberry bed ;
Her neck, like to a bunch of Columbines ;
Her breast, like Lilies ere their leaves be shed ;
Her nipples, like young blossomed Jessamines :
    Such fragrant flowers do give most odorous smell ;
    But her sweet odour did them all excel.

SPENSER.

LOVE-LETTERS MADE OF FLOWERS

ON A PRINT OF ONE OF THEM IN A BOOK

AN exquisite invention this,
Worthy of Love's most honied kiss,
This art of writing *billets-doux*
In buds, and odours, and bright hues !
In saying all one feels and thinks
In clever daffodils and pinks ;
In puns of tulips ; and in phrases,
Charming for their truth, of daisies ;
Uttering, as well as silence may,
The sweetest words the sweetest way.
How fit too for the lady's bosom !
The place where *billets-doux* repose 'em.

    What delight, in some sweet spot
Combining *love* with *garden* plot,
At once to cultivate one's flowers
And one's epistolary powers !
Growing one's own choice words and fancies
In orange tubs, and beds of pansies ;
One's sighs and passionate declarations
In odorous rhetoric of carnations ;

22

BLACK-EYED DAISIES

Seeing how far one's stocks will reach ;
Taking due care one's flowers of speech
To guard from blight as well as bathos,
And watering, every day, one's pathos !

A letter comes, just gather'd.   We
Dote on its tender brilliancy ;
Inhale its delicate expressions
Of balm and pea, and its confessions
Made with as sweet a *Maiden's Blush*
As ever morn bedew'd on bush
('Tis in reply to one of ours,
Made of the most convincing flowers),
Then after we have kissed its wit
And heart, in water putting it
(To keep its remarks fresh), go round
Our little eloquent plot of ground,
And with enchanted hands compose
Our answer all of lily and rose,
Of tuberose and of violet,
And *Little Darling* (Mignonette),
Of *Look at me* and *Call me to you*
(Words that while they greet go through you),
Of *Thoughts*, of *Flames*, *Forget-me-not*,
Bridewort,—in short, the whole blest lot
Of vouchers for a life-long kiss
And literally, breathing bliss.

LEIGH HUNT.

THE SEEDS OF LOVE

I SOW'D the seeds of love,
 It was all in the spring,
In April, May, and sunny June,
 When small birds they do sing.

My garden was planted full
 Of flowers everywhere,
But for myself I could not choose
 The flower I held so dear.

My gardener was standing by,
 And he would choose for me ;
He chose the primrose, the lily and pink,
 But those I refused all three.

The primrose I did reject,
 Because it came too soon ;
The lily and the pink I overlook'd,
 And vow'd I would wait till June.

In June came the rose so red,
 And that 's the flower for me ;
But when I gathered the rose so dear
 I gained but the willow tree.

Oh, the willow tree will twist,
 And the willow tree will twine ;
And would I were in the young man's arms,
 That ever has this heart of mine.

My gardener, as he stood by,
 He bade me take great care,
For if I gathered the rose so red,
 There groweth up a sharp thorn there.

FLOWERS OF DAWN

D

I told him I 'd take no care,
  Till I did feel the smart,
And still did press the thorn so dear
  Till the thorn did pierce my heart.

A posy of hyssop I 'll make,
  No other flower I 'll touch,
That all the world may plainly see
  I love one flower too much.

My garden is now run wild ;
  When I shall plant anew,
My bed, that once was filled with thyme,
  Is now o'errun with rue.

ANON.

TO EMILIA VIVIANI

MADONNA, wherefore hast thou sent to me
    Sweet-basil and mignonette,
    Embleming love and health, which never yet
In the same wreath might be ?
    Alas, and they are wet !
Is it with thy kisses or thy tears ?
        For never rain or dew
        Such fragrance drew
From plant or flower—the very doubt endears
        My sadness ever new,
The sighs I breathe, the tears I shed for thee.
Send the stars light, but send not love to me,
    In whom love ever made
Health like a heap of embers soon to fade.

SHELLEY.

REMEMBRANCE

SWIFTER far than summer's flight—
Swifter far than youth's delight—
Swifter far than happy night,
    Art thou come and gone—
As the earth when leaves are dead,
As the night when sleep is sped,
As the heart when joy is fled,
    I am left lone, alone.

The swallow summer comes again—
The owlet night resumes her reign—
But the wild-swan youth is fain
    To fly with thee, false as thou.—
My heart each day desires the morrow,
Sleep itself is turned to sorrow;
Vainly would my winter borrow
    Sunny leaves from any bough.

Lilies for a bridal bed—
Roses for a matron's head—
Violets for a maiden dead—
    Pansies let my flowers be:
On the living grave I bear
Scatter them without a tear—
Let no friend, however dear,
    Waste one hope, one fear for me.

SHELLEY.

MAY TIME

THYRSIS and Milla, arm in arm together,
In merry may-time to the green garden walked,
Where all the way they wanton riddles talked ;
The youthful boy, kissing her cheeks so rosy,
Beseeched her there to gather him a posy.
She straight her light green silken coats uptucked,
And may for Mill and thyme for Thyrsis plucked ;
Which when she brought, he clasped her by the
        middle
And kissed her sweet, but could not read her riddle.
' Ah, fool ! ' with that the nymph set up a laughter,
And blushed, and ran away, and he ran after.

THOMAS MORLEY.

THERE IS A GARDEN IN HER FACE

THERE is a garden in her face
Where roses and white lilies grow ;
A heavenly paradise is that place
Wherein all pleasant fruits do grow.
    There cherries grow which none may buy,
    Till ' Cherry ripe ' themselves do cry.

Those cherries fairly do enclose
Of orient pearl a double row,
Which when her lovely laughter shows,
They look like rosebuds filled with snow ;
    Yet them nor peer nor prince can buy,
    Till ' Cherry ripe ' themselves do cry.

27

Her eyes like angels watch them still,
Her brows like bended bows do stand,
Threatening with piercing frowns to kill
All that attempt, with eye or hand,
    Those sacred cherries to come nigh
    Till ' Cherry ripe ' themselves do cry.
THOMAS CAMPION.

A SONG

ASK me no more where Jove bestows,
When June is past, the fading rose ;
For in your beauty's orient deep
These flowers, as in their causes, sleep.

Ask me no more whither do stray
The golden atoms of the day ;
For in pure love heaven did prepare
Those powders to enrich your hair.

Ask me no more whither doth haste
The nightingale when May is past ;
For in your sweet dividing throat
She winters and keeps warm her note.

Ask me no more where those stars 'light,
That downwards fall in dead of night ;
For in your eyes they sit, and there
Fixed become, as in their sphere.

Ask me no more if east or west
The phœnix builds her spicy nest,
For unto you at last she flies.
And in your fragrant bosom dies.
CAREW.

28

A GARDEN FANCY

HERE'S the garden she walked across,
  Arm in my arm, such a short while since :
Hark, now I push its wicket, the moss
  Hinders the hinges and makes them wince !
She must have reached this shrub ere she turned,
  As back with that murmur the wicket swung ;
For she laid the poor snail, my chance foot spurned,
  To feed and forget it the leaves among.

Down this side of the gravel-walk
  She went while her robe's edge brushed the box :
And here she paused in her gracious talk
  To point me a moth on the milk-white phlox.
Roses ranged in a valiant row,
  I will never think that she passed you by !
She loves you, noble roses, I know ;
  But yonder, see, where the rock-plants lie !

This flower she stopped at, finger on lip,
  Stooped over in doubt, as settling its claim ;
Till she gave me, with pride to make no slip,
  Its soft meandering Spanish name :
What a name ! Was it love or praise ?
  Speech half-asleep or song half-awake ?
I must learn Spanish, one of these days,
  Only for that slow sweet name's sake.

Roses, if I live and do well,
  I may bring her, one of these days,
To fix you fast with as fine a spell,
  Fit you each with his Spanish phrase ;

29

But do not detain me now ; for she lingers
  There, like sunshine over the ground,
And ever I see her soft white fingers
  Searching after the bud she found.

Flower, you Spaniard, look that you grow not,
  Stay as you are, and be loved for ever !
Bud, if I kiss you 'tis that you blow not :
  Mind, the shut pink mouth opens never !
For while it pouts, her fingers wrestle,
  Twinkling the audacious leaves between,
Till round they turn and down they nestle—
  Is not the dear mark still to be seen ?

Where I find her not, beauties vanish ;
  Whither I follow her, beauties flee ;
Is there no method to tell her in Spanish
  June's twice June since she breathed it with me ?
Come, bud, show me the least of her traces,
  Treasure my lady's lightest footfall !
—Ah, you may flout and turn up your faces—
  Roses, you are not so fair after all !

BROWNING.

SNAPDRAGON

SHE bade me follow to her garden where
  The mellow sunlight stood as in a cup
Between the old grey walls ; I did not dare
  To raise my face, I did not dare look up
  Lest her bright eyes like sparrows should fly in
  My windows of discovery and shrill ' Sin ! '

BLUE   DELPHINIUMS

So with a downcast mien and laughing voice
I followed, followed the swing of her white dress
That rocked in a lilt along : I watched the poise
Of her feet as they flew for a space, then paused to press
The grass deep down with the royal burden of her :
And gladly I 'd offered my breast to the tread of her.

' I like to see,' she said, and she crouched her down,
She sunk into my sight like a settling bird ;
And her bosom couched in the confines of her gown
Like heavy birds at rest there, softly stirred
By her measured breaths : ' I like to see,' said she,
' The snapdragon put out his tongue at me.'
She laughed, she reached her hand out to the flower,
Closing its crimson throat : my own throat in her power
Strangled, my heart swelled up so full
As if it would burst its wineskin in my throat,
Choke me in my own crimson ; I watched her pull
The gorge of the gaping flower, till the blood did
    float

Over my eyes and I was blind—
Her large brown hand stretched over
The windows of my mind,
And in the dark I did discover
Things I was out to find :
My grail, a brown bowl twined
With swollen veins that met in the wrist,
Under whose brown the amethyst
I longed to taste : and I longed to turn
My heart's red measure in her cup,
I longed to feel my hot blood burn
With the lambent amethyst in her cup.

Then suddenly she looked up
And I was blind in a tawny-gold day
Till she took her eyes away.

So she came down from above
And emptied my heart of love . . .
So I held my heart aloft
To the cuckoo that fluttered above,
And she settled soft.

It seemed that I and the morning world
Were pressed cup-shape to take this reiver
Bird who was weary to have furled
Her wings on us,
As we were weary to receive her :

This bird, this rich
Sumptuous central grain,
This mutable witch,
This one refrain,
This laugh in the fight,
This clot of light,
This core of night.

She spoke, and I closed my eyes
To shut hallucinations out.
I echoed with surprise
Hearing my mere lips shout
The answer they did devise.

Again, I saw a brown bird hover
Over the flowers at my feet ;
I felt a brown bird hover ,
Over my heart, and sweet

32

Its shadow lay on my heart ;
I thought I saw on the clover
A brown bee pulling apart
The closed flesh of the clover
And burrowing in its heart.

She moved her hand, and again
I felt the brown bird hover
Over my heart . . . and then
The bird came down on my heart,
As on a nest the rover
Cuckoo comes, and shoves over
The brim each careful part
Of love, takes possession and settles her down,
With her wings and her feathers does drown
The nest in a heat of love.

She turned her flushed face to me for the glint
Of a moment.   ' See,' she laughed, ' if you also
Can make them yawn.'   I put my hand to the dint
In the flower's throat, and the flower gaped wide with
        woe.
She watched, she went of a sudden intensely still,
She watched my hand, and I let her watch her fill.

I pressed the wretched, throttled flower between
My fingers, till its head lay back, its fangs
Poised at her : like a weapon my hand stood white and
        keen,
And I held the choked flower-serpent in its pangs
Of mordant anguish till she ceased to laugh,
Until her pride's flag, smitten, cleaved down to the
        staff.

E

She hid her face, she murmured between her lips
The low word 'Don't!'   I let the flower fall,
But held my hand afloat still towards the slips
Of blossom she fingered, and my crisp fingers all
Put forth to her : she did not move, nor I,
For my hand like a snake watched hers that could
       not fly.
Then I laughed in the dark of my heart, I did exult
Like a sudden chuckling of music : I bade her eyes
Meet mine, I opened her helpless eyes to consult
Their fear, their shame, their joy that underlies
Defeat in such a battle : in the dark of her eyes
My heart was fierce to make her laughter rise . . .
Till her dark deeps shook with convulsive thrills, and
       the dark
Of her spirit wavered like water thrilled with light,
And my heart leaped up in a longing to plunge its stark
Fervour within the pool of her twilight :
Within her spacious gloom, in the mystery
Of her barbarous soul, to grope with ecstasy . . .

And I do not care though the large hands of revenge
Shall get my throat at last—shall get it soon,
If the joy that they are lifted to avenge
Have risen red on my night as a harvest moon,
Which even death can only put out for me,
And death I know is better than not-to-be.

D. H. LAWRENCE.

HEART'S-EASE

THERE is a flower I wish to wear,
  But not until first worn by you . . .
Heart's-ease . . . of all earth's flowers most rare ;
  Bring it ; and bring enough for two.

LANDOR.

TO THE CYCLAMEN

THOU Cyclamen of crumpled horn,
  Toss not thy head aside ;
Repose it where the Loves were born,
  In that warm dell abide.
Whatever flowers, on mountain, field,
  Or garden, may arise,
Thine only that pure odour yield
  Which never can suffice.
Emblem of her I 've loved so long,
Go, carry her this little song.

LANDOR.

HOW PANSIES, OR HEART'S-EASE, CAME FIRST

FROLIC virgins once these were,
Over-loving, living here :
Being here their ends denied,
Ran for sweethearts mad, and died.
Love, in pity of their tears,
And their loss in blooming years,
For their restless here-spent hours,
Gave them heart's-ease turned to flowers.

HERRICK.

35

A LEGEND OF CHERRIES

NOW, St. Joseph's cottage stood
Close beside a cherry wood,

And, what time the trees grew red
With their luscious fruit, 'tis said,

Jesus, at His mother's gown,
Begged to have the branches down :

All in vain she made reply,
' Mother cannot reach so high,'

For He begged them none the less,
In His perfect childishness.

Joseph, in his workshop near,
Heard the Babe and would not hear,

Heard the Blessed Virgin say,
' Joseph, pull them down, I pray ! '

But he answered, with a frown,
' Let His Father pull them down.'

Then, to his great wonderment,
Every cherry branch was bent,

And Our Lady sweetly smiled,
Picking cherries for her Child.

CHARLES DALMON.

EVE

EVE, with her basket, was
Deep in the bells and grass,
Wading in bells and grass
Up to her knees,
Picking a dish of sweet
Berries and plums to eat,
Down in the bells and grass
Under the trees.

Mute as a mouse in a
Corner the cobra lay,
Curled round the bough of the
Cinnamon tall . . .
Now to get even and
Humble proud heaven and
Now was the moment or
Never at all.

'Eva !'   Each syllable
Light as a flower fell,
'Eva !' he whispered the
Wondering maid,
Soft as a bubble sung
Out of a linnet's lung,
Soft and most silverly
'Eva !' he said.

Picture that orchard sprite,
Eve, with her body white,
Supple and smooth to her

Slim finger tips,
Wondering, listening,
Eve with a berry
Half-way to her lips.

Oh had our simple Eve
Seen through the make-believe !
Had she but known the
Pretender he was !
Out of the boughs he came,
Whispering still her name,
Tumbling in twenty rings
Into the grass.

Here was the strangest pair
In the world anywhere,
Eve in the bells and grass
Kneeling, and he
Telling his story low . . .
Singing birds saw them go
Down the dark path to
The blasphemous Tree.

Oh what a clatter when
Titmouse and Jenny Wren
Saw him successful and
Taking his leave !
How the birds rated him,
How they all hated him !
How they all pitied
Poor motherless Eve !

Picture her crying
Outside in the lane,

Eve, with no dish of sweet
Berries and plums to eat,
Haunting the gate of the
Orchard in vain . . .
Picture the lewd delight
Under the hill to-night—
' Eva ! ' the toast goes round,
' Eva ! ' again.

RALPH HODGSON.

THE CHILD IN THE STORY
AWAKES

THE light of dawn rose on my dreams
    And from afar I seemed to hear
In sleep the mellow blackbird call
    Hollow and sweet and clear.

I prythee, Nurse, my casement open,
    Wildly the garden peals with singing,
And hooting through the dewy pines
    The goblins all are winging.

O listen the droning of the bees,
    That in the roses take delight !
And see a cloud stays in the blue
    Like an angel still and bright.

The gentle sky is spread like silk,
    And, Nurse, the moon doth languish there,
As if it were a perfect jewel
    In the morning's soft-spun hair.

39

The greyness of the distant hills
　　Is silvered in the lucid East,
See, now the sheeny plumèd cock
　　Wags haughtily his crest.

' O come you out, O come you out,
　　Lily, and lavender, and lime ;
The kingcup swings his golden bell,
　　And plumpy cherries drum the time.

' O come you out, O come you out,
　　Roses, and dew, and mignonette ;
The sun is in the steep blue sky,
　　Sweetly the morning star is set.'

WALTER DE LA MARE.

THE THIEF

WHEN the paths of dream were mist-muffled,
　　And the hours were dim and small
(Through still nights on wet orchard grass
　　Like rain the apples fall),
Then naked-footed, secretly,
　　The thief dropped over the wall.

Apple-boughs spattered mist at him,
　　The dawn was as cold as death,
With a stealthy joy at the heart of it,
　　And the stir of a small sweet breath,
And a robin breaking his heart on song
　　As a young child sorroweth.

40

BEES WITH THE PLUSHY AND
PLAUSIBLE NOSES'

The thief's feet bruised wet lavender
  Into sweet sharp surprise ;
The orchard, full of pears and joy,
  Smiled like a gold sunrise ;
But the blind house stared down on him
  With strange, white-lidded eyes.

He stood at the world's secret heart
  In the haze-wrapt mystery ;
And fat pears, mellow on the lip,
  He supped like a honey-bee ;
But the apples he crunched with sharp white teeth
  Were pungent, like the sea.

And this was the oldest garden joy,
  Living and young and sweet.
And the melting mists took radiance,
  And the silence a rhythmic beat,
For the day came stealing stealthily,
  A thief, upon furtive feet.

And the walls that ring this world about
  Quivered like gossamer,
Till he heard, in the other worlds beyond,
  The other peoples stir,
And met strange, sudden, shifting eyes
  Through the filmy barrier. . . .

                              ROSE MACAULAY.

THE TUFT OF FLOWERS

I WENT to turn the grass once after one
Who mowed it in the dew before the sun.

The dew was gone that made his blade so keen
Before I came to view the levelled scene.

I looked for him behind an isle of trees ;
I listened for his whetstone on the breeze.

But he had gone his way, the grass all mown,
And I must be, as he had been,—alone.

' As all must be,' I said within my heart,
' Whether they work together or apart.'

But as I said it, swift there passed me by
On noiseless wing a 'wildered butterfly,

Seeking with memories grown dim o'er night
Some resting flower of yesterday's delight.

And once I marked his flight go round and round,
As where some flower lay withering on the ground.

And then he flew as far as eye could see,
And then on tremulous wing came back to me.

I thought of questions that have no reply,
And would have turned to toss the grass to dry ;

But he turned first, and led my eye to look
At a tall tuft of flowers beside a brook,

42

SWEET LAVENDER

A leaping tongue of bloom the scythe had spared
Beside a reedy brook the scythe had bared.

I left my place to know them by their name,
Finding them butterfly weed when I came.

The mower in the dew had loved them thus,
By leaving them to flourish, not for us,

Nor yet to draw one thought of ours to him,
But from sheer morning gladness at the brim.

The butterfly and I had lit upon,
Nevertheless, a message from the dawn,

That made me hear the wakening birds around,
And hear his long scythe whispering to the ground,

And feel a spirit kindred to my own ;
So that henceforth I worked no more alone ;

But glad with him, I worked as with his aid,
And weary, sought at noon with him the shade ;

And dreaming, as it were, held brotherly speech
With one whose thought I had not hoped to reach.

' Men work together,' I told him from my heart,
' Whether they work together or apart.'

ROBERT FROST.

THE PRIMROSE

NO more, from now, called pale and wan,
    As though a pitiful weak thing :
A sickly offspring of weak Sun
    And youngish Spring.

Thy father's golden skin is thine,
    And his eye's gleam ; but his bold rays
Are tempered by thy mother's blood
    To softer ways.

For thou hast made the banks ooze gold,
    And made old woods their darkness break ;
In them I would not fall at night,
    Wert thou awake.

Here is the Primrose family :
    The first born is full blown and tall ;
Two in half bloom just reach his chin,
    Three are buds small.

Then, since the first born healthy seems—
    No drooping one I 've chanced upon—
It would be speaking false to call
    Them pale and wan.

They mean the Primrose plucked and withered,
    Not growing in his golden shine,
Who 'd prove by him how Phyllis looks
    When she doth pine.

44

BLACKTHORN AND A BLUE BUTTERFLY

Indeed, where find a hardier flower ?
  Born when the Spring wind chilly blows,
Still beautiful in Summer's days—
  O rare Primrose !

WILLIAM H. DAVIES.

TO VIOLETS

WELCOME, maids of honour,
  You do bring
  In the spring,
And wait upon her.

She has virgins many,
  Fresh and fair ;
  Yet you are
More sweet than any.

You 're the maiden posies,
  And so graced
  To be placed
'Fore damask roses.

Yet though thus respected,
  By-and-by
  Ye do lie,
Poor girls, neglected.

HERRICK.

'THE HAWTHORN HATH A DEATHLY SMELL'

THE flowers of the field
  Have a sweet smell ;
Meadowsweet, tansy, thyme,
  And faint-heart pimpernel ;
But sweeter even than these,
  The silver of the may
Wreathed is with incense for
  The Judgment Day.

An apple, a child, dust,
  When falls the evening rain,
Wild briar's spiced leaves,
  Breathe memories again ;
With further memory fraught,
  The silver of the may
Wreathed is with incense for
  The Judgment Day.

Eyes of all loveliness—
  Shadow of strange delight,
Even as a flower fades
  Must thou from sight ;
But oh, o'er thy grave's mound,
  Till come the Judgment Day,
Wreathed shall with incense be
  Thy sharp-thorned may.

WALTER DE LA MARE.

WILD VIOLETS

TO DAFFODILS

FAIR Daffodils, we weep to see
   You haste away so soon ;
As yet the early-rising sun
   Has not attained his noon.
      Stay, stay,
    Until the hasting day
      Has run
    But to the evensong ;
And, having prayed together, we
   Will go with you along.

We have short time to stay, as you,
   We have as short a spring ;
As quick a growth to meet decay,
   As you or anything.
      We die
    As your hours do, and dry
      Away,
    Like to the summer's rain ;
Or as the pearls of morning's dew,
   Ne'er to be found again.

                      HERRICK.

A SONG OF APPLE-BLUTH

HAVE you ne'er waked in the grey of the day-dawn
Whitely to stand at the window scarce-seen,
Over the garden to peer in the May-dawn
Past to the fruit-close whose pale boughs not green

Slowly reveal a fresh faintness a-flutter
White to the young grass and pink to the sky ?
O, then a low call to waking we utter,
' Bluth, lasses, apple-bluth spirts low and high.'

Out, lasses, out, to the apple-garth hasten—
Nay, never tarry to net your glad hair—
Here are no lovers your kissed shoes to fasten
(O, for the days when girls' feet may go bare).
Over the dim lawn the May-rime yet lingers
Pallid and dark as the down of the dawn—
Gather your skirts in your delicate fingers,
Stoop as you run o'er the almond-hung lawn.

Look through the trees ere dawn's twilight is over—
Lo, how the light boughs seem lost in the stars ;
Everywhere bluth the grey sky seems to cover,
Quivering and scented, new spring's kisses' scars.
Wet are the blossoms to wash your faint faces—
Bury your faces cheek-deep in their chill ;
Press the flushed petals and open your dresses,—
So—let them trickle your young breasts to thrill.

Winter has wronged us of sunlight and sweetness,
We who so soon must be hid from the sun ;
Winter is on us as Summer's completeness
Faint-hearted drops down a tired world undone ;
Brief is the bloom-time as sleepy maids' laughter
Who know not one bed-time 'tis Summer's last day,
Though from the heart of the rose they have quaffed
    her—
Come, lasses, come, ere our rose-world falls grey.
                        GORDON BOTTOMLEY.

48

THE DUEL

EVENING PRIMROSE

WHEN the sun sinks in the west,
And dew-drops pearl the Evening's breast ;
Almost as pale as moonbeams are,
Or its companionable star,
The Evening Primrose opes anew
Its delicate blossoms to the dew ;
And hermit-like, shunning the light,
Wastes its fair bloom upon the Night ;
Who, blindfold to its fond caresses,
Knows not the beauty he possesses.
Thus it blooms on while Night is by ;
When Day looks out with open eye,
'Bashed at the gaze it cannot shun,
It faints, and withers, and is gone.

JOHN CLARE.

ROSE OF SHARON

GO, pretty child, and bear this flower
Unto thy little Saviour ;
And tell him, by that bud now blown,
He is the Rose of Sharon known.
When thou hast said so, stick it there
Upon his bib or stomacher ;
And tell him, for good handsel too,
That thou hast brought a whistle new,
Made of a clean straight oaten reed,
To charm his cries at time of need.
Tell him, for coral thou hast none,
But if thou hadst, he should have one ;

49

But poor thou art, and known to be
Even as moneyless as he.
Lastly, if thou canst win a kiss
From those mellifluous lips of his ;
Then never take a second on,
To spoil the first impression.

HERRICK.

BEANS IN BLOSSOM

THE south-west wind ! how pleasant in the face
It breathes ! while, sauntering in a musing pace,
I roam these new ploughed fields ; or by the side
Of this old wood, where happy birds abide,
And the rich blackbird through his golden bill,
Utters wild music when the rest are still.
Luscious the scent comes of the blossomed bean,
As o'er the path in rich disorder lean
Its stalks ; whence bees, in busy rows and toils,
Load home luxuriantly their yellow spoils.
The herd-cows toss the molehills in their play ;
And often stand the stranger's steps at bay,
Mid clover blossoms red and tawny white,
Strong scented with the summer's warm delight.

JOHN CLARE.

THE WOOD-SPURGE

THE wind flapped loose, the wind was still,
Shaken out dead from tree and hill :
I had walked on at the wind's will,—
I sat now, for the wind was still.

50

ROSE OF APRIL

Between my knees my forehead was,—
My lips drawn in, said not Alas !
My hair was over in the grass,
My naked ears heard the day pass.

My eyes, wide open, had the run
Of some ten weeds to fix upon ;
Among those few, out of the sun,
The wood-spurge flowered, three cups in one.

From perfect grief there need not be
Wisdom or even memory :
One thing then learnt remains to me,—
The wood-spurge has a cup of three.

ROSSETTI.

THE SUN-FLOWER

AH, Sun-flower ! weary of time,
Who countest the steps of the sun ;
Seeking after that sweet golden clime,
Where the traveller's journey is done ;

Where the Youth pined away with desire,
And the pale Virgin shrouded in snow,
Arise from their graves, and aspire
Where my Sun-flower wishes to go.

BLAKE.

THE POPPY

TO MONICA

SUMMER set lip to earth's bosom bare,
And left the flushed print in a poppy there :
Like a yawn of fire from the grass it came,
And the fanning wind puffed it to flapping flame.

With burnt mouth, red like a lion's, it drank
The blood of the sun as he slaughtered sank,
And dipped its cup in the purpurate shine
When the eastern conduits ran with wine.

Till it grew lethargied with fierce bliss,
And hot as a swinked gipsy is,
And drowsed in sleepy savageries,
With mouth wide a-pout for a sultry kiss.

A child and man paced side by side,
Treading the skirts of eventide ;
But between the clasp of his hand and hers
Lay, felt not, twenty withered years.

She turned, with the rout of her dusk South hair,
And saw the sleeping gipsy there ;
And snatched and snapped it in swift child's whim,
With—' Keep it, long as you live ! '—to him.

And his smile, as nymphs from their laving meres,
Trembled up from a bath of tears ;
And joy, like a mew sea-rocked apart,
Tossed on the waves of his troubled heart.

52

For *he* saw what she did not see,
That—as kindled by its own fervency—
The verge shrivelled inward smoulderingly :
And suddenly 'twixt his hand and hers
He knew the twenty withered years—
No flower, but twenty shrivelled years.

' Was never such thing until this hour,'
Low to his heart he said ; ' the flower
Of sleep brings wakening to me,
And of oblivion memory.'

' Was never this thing to me,' he said,
' Though with bruised poppies my feet are red ! '
And again to his own heart very low :
' O child ! I love, for I love and know ;

' But you, who love nor know at all
The diverse chambers in Love's guest-hall,
Where some rise early, few sit long :
In how different accents hear the throng
His great Pentecostal tongue ;

' Who know not love from amity,
Nor my reported self from me ;
A fair fit gift is this, meseems,
You give—this withering flower of dreams.

' O frankly fickle, and fickly true,
Do you know what the days will do to you ?
To your love and you what the days will do,
O frankly fickle, and fickly true ?

53

'You have loved me, Fair, three lives—or days :
'Twill pass with the passing of my face.
But where *I* go your face goes too,
To watch lest I play false to you.

'I am but, my sweet, your foster-lover,
Knowing well when certain years are over
You vanish from me to another ;
Yet I know, and love, like the foster-mother.

'So, frankly fickle, and fickly true !
For my brief life-while I take from you
This token, fair and fit, meseems,
For me—this withering flower of dreams.'

The sleep-flower sways in the wheat its head,
Heavy with dreams, as that with bread :
The goodly grain and the sun-flushed sleeper
The reaper reaps, and Time the reaper.

I hang 'mid men my needless head,
And my fruit is dreams, as theirs is bread :
The goodly men and the sun-hazed sleeper
Time shall reap, but after the reaper
The world shall glean of me, the sleeper.

Love, love ! your flower of withered dream
In leavèd rhyme lies safe, I deem,
Sheltered and shut in a nook of rhyme,
From the reaper man, and his reaper Time.

Love ! *I* fall into the claws of Time :
But lasts within a leavèd rhyme
All that the world of me esteems—
My withered dreams, my withered dreams.

FRANCIS THOMPSON.

54

DAISIES AND DELPHINIUMS

THE DAISY

I KNOW not why thy beauty should
   Remind me of the cold, dark grave—
Thou Flower, as fair as Moonlight, when
   She kissed the mouth of a black Cave.

All other Flowers can coax the Bees,
   All other Flowers are sought but thee :
Dost thou remind them all of Death,
   Sweet Flower, as thou remindest me ?

Thou seemest like a blessed ghost,
   So white, so cold, though crowned with gold ;
Among these glazed Buttercups,
   And purple Thistles, rough and bold.

When I am dead, nor thought of more,
   Out of all human memory—
Grow you on my forsaken grave,
   And win for me a stranger's sigh.

A day or two the lilies fade ;
   A month, ay less, no friends are seen :
Then, claimant to forgotten graves,
   Share my lost place with the wild green.

                         WILLIAM H. DAVIES.

A WIDOW'S WEEDS

A POOR old Widow in her weeds
   Sowed her garden with wild-flower seeds ;
Not too shallow, and not too deep,
And down came April—drip—drip—drip.

55

Up shone May, like gold, and soon
Green as an arbour grew leafy June.
And now all summer she sits and sews
Where willow herb, comfrey, bugloss blows,
Teasle and tansy, meadowsweet,
Campion, toadflax, and rough hawksbit ;
Brown bee orchis, and Peals of Bells ;
Clover, burnet, and thyme she smells ;
Like Oberon's meadows her garden is
Drowsy from dawn till dusk with bees.
Weeps she never, but sometimes sighs,
And peeps at her garden with bright brown eyes ;
And all she has is all she needs—
A poor old Widow in her weeds.

WALTER DE LA MARE.

THE GARDEN IN SEPTEMBER

NOW thin mists temper the slow-ripening beams
Of the September sun : his golden gleams
On gaudy flowers shine, that prank the rows
Of high-grown hollyhocks, and all tall shows
That Autumn flaunteth in his bushy bowers ;
Where tomtits hanging from the drooping heads
Of giant sun-flowers, peck the nutty seeds ;
And in the feathery aster bees on wing
Seize and set free the honied flowers,
Till thousand stars leap with their visiting :
While ever across the path mazily flit,
Unpiloted in the sun,
The dreamy butterflies
With dazzling colours powdered and soft glooms,

56

TOAD-FLAX

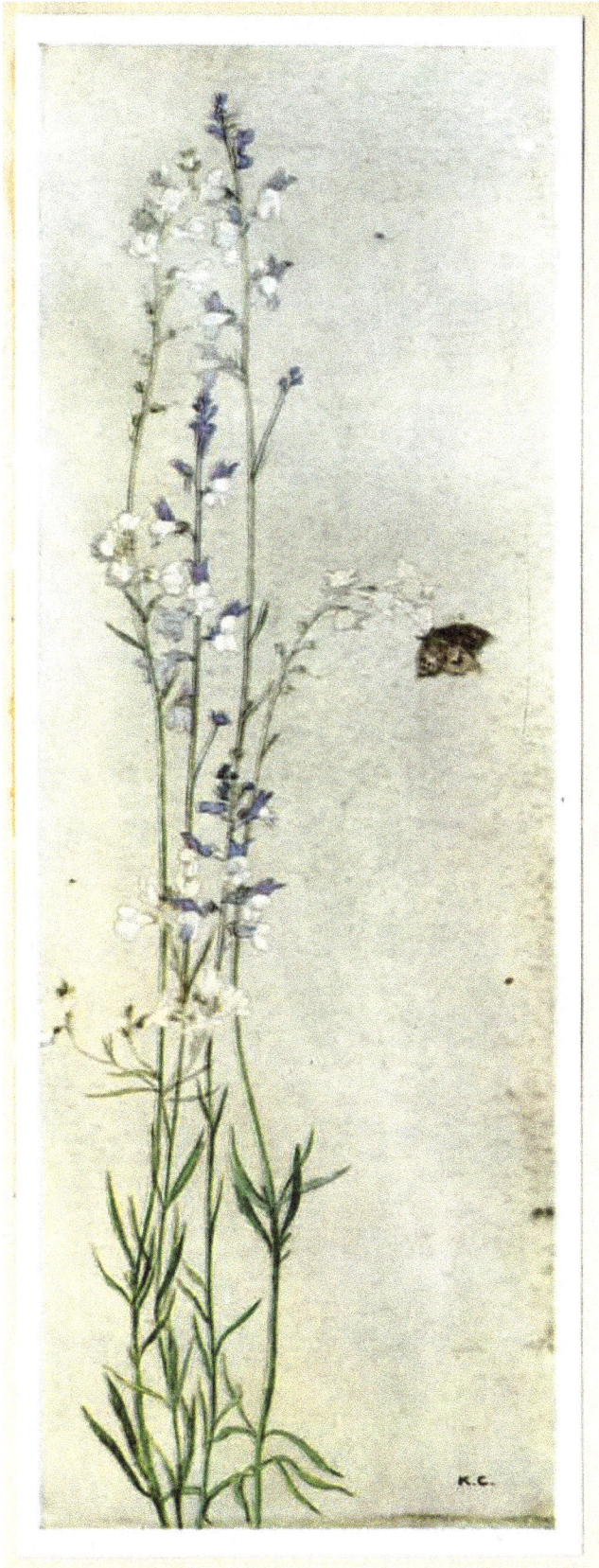

White, black and crimson stripes, and peacock eyes,
Or on chance flowers sit,
With idle effort plundering one by one
The nectaries of deepest throated blooms.

With gentle flaws the western breeze
Into the garden saileth,
Scarce here and there stirring the single trees,
For his sharpness he vaileth :
So long a comrade of the bearded corn,
Now from the stubbles whence the shocks are borne,
O'er dewy lawns he turns to stray,
As mindful of the kisses and soft play
Wherewith he enamoured the light-hearted May,
Ere he deserted her ;
Lover of fragrance, and too late repents ;
Nor more of heavy hyacinth now may drink,
Nor spicy pink,
Nor Summer's rose, nor garnered lavender,
But the few lingering scents
Of streakèd pea, and gillyflower, and stocks
Of courtly purple, and aromatic phlox.

And at all times to hear are drowsy tones
Of dizzy flies, and humming drones,
With sudden flap of pigeon wings in the sky,
Or the wild cry
Of thirsty rooks, that scour ascare
The distant blue, to watering as they fare
With creaking pinions, or—on business bent,
If aught their ancient polity displease—
Come gathering to their colony, and there
Settling in ragged parliament,
Some stormy council hold in the high trees.

ROBERT BRIDGES.

57

SEA-COUNTRY

BID me by poppied fields again,
Drift-campion and the seeded snow
In wealden hollows lulled and lain
From the wind's torment let me go ;

Came ever inland peace so near
These storm-ports of the watery globe ?
Here is the salt-sown pine and here
The snake-stems wear a whispering robe.

These coverts, paved with rushy green,
Were planted for the turtle's bower,
And faintly hums the breeze between
Crab-orchard and sea-pasturing flower :

Here, in his twisted arbour-pale,
The marsh-bird warbles, as the sea
Had lent his voice a sail,
And wave-drops for fresh melody.

'Tis the lark's race ; did he not win
The rippling steps of music's throne,
How clear, the dancing wave within,
Were heard, how many a voice less known ;

How many a voice, ere this one slake
His thirst with cup that music yields,
And on the desert silence break,
And not these fields, and not these fields.

VIVIAN LOCKE ELLIS.

58

ALLONGIA

THE BLUEBELL

THE Bluebell is the sweetest flower
    That waves in summer air :
Its blossoms have the mightiest power
    To soothe my spirit's care.

There is a spell in purple heath
    Too wildly, sadly dear ;
The violet has a fragrant breath,
    But fragrance will not cheer.

The trees are bare, the sun is cold,
    And seldom, seldom seen ;
The heavens have lost their zone of gold
    And earth her robe of green.

And ice upon the glancing stream
    Has cast its sombre shade ;
And distant hills and valleys seem
    In frozen mist arrayed.

The Bluebell cannot charm me now,
    The heath has lost its bloom ;
The violets in the glen below,
    They yield no sweet perfume.

But, though I mourn the sweet Bluebell,
    'Tis better far away ;
I know how fast my tears would swell
    To see it smile to-day.

For, oh ! when chill the sunbeams fall
  Adown that dreary sky,
And gild yon dank and darkened wall
  With transient brilliancy,

How do I weep, how do I pine
  For the time of flowers to come,
And turn me from that fading shine,
  To mourn the fields of home !

EMILY BRONTË.

THE LILAC

DEAR lilac-tree, a-spreadèn wide
Thy purple blooth on ev'ry zide,
As if the hollow sky did shed
Its blue upon thy flow'ry head ;
Oh ! whether I mid sheäre wi' thee
Thy open aïr, my bloomèn tree,
Or zee thy blossoms vrom the gloom,
'Ithin my zunless workèn-room,
My heart do leäp, but leäp wi' sighs,
At zight o' thee avore my eyes,
For when thy grey-blue head do swäy
In cloudless light, 'tis Spring, 'tis Mäy.

'Tis Spring, 'tis Mäy, as Mäy woonce shed
His glowèn light above my head—
When thy green boughs, wi' bloomy tips,
Did sheäde my childern's laughèn lips ;
A screenèn vrom the noonday gleäre
Their rwosy cheaks an' glossy heäir ;
The while their mother's needle sped,
Too quick vor zight, the snow-white thread,

Unless her han', wi' lovèn ceäre,
Did smoothe their little heads o' heäir ;
Or wi' a sheäke, tie up anew
Vor zome wild voot, a slippèn shoe ;
An' I did lean bezide thy mound,
Ageän the deäsy-dappled ground,
The while the woaken clock did tick
My hour o' rest away too quick,
An' call me off to work anew,
Wi' slowly-ringèn strokes, woone, two.

Zoo let me zee noo darksome cloud
Bedim to-day thy flow'ry sh'oud,
But let en bloom on ev'ry spräy,
Drough all the days o' zunny Mäy.

WILLIAM BARNES.

THE MOSS-ROSE

WALKING to-day in your garden, O gracious lady,
Little you thought as you turned in that alley
remote and shady,
And gave me a rose and asked if I knew its savour—
The old-world scent of the moss-rose, flower of a
bygone favour—

Little you thought as you waited the word of
appraisement,
Laughing at first and then amazed at my amaze-
ment,
That the rose you gave was a gift already cherished,
And the garden whence you plucked it a garden long
perished.

I

But I—I saw that garden, with its one treasure
The tiny moss-rose, tiny even by childhood's measure,
And the long morning shadow of the dusty laurel,
And a boy and a girl beneath it, flushed with a childish
    quarrel.

She wept for one little bud : but he, outreaching
The hand of brotherly right, would take it for all her
    beseeching :
And she flung her arms about him, and gave like a
    sister,
And laughed at her own tears, and wept again when he
    kissed her.

So the rose is mine long since, and whenever I find it
And drink again the sharp sweet scent of the moss
    behind it,
I remember the tears of a child, and her love and her
    laughter,
And the morning shadows of youth and the night that
    fell thereafter.

HENRY NEWBOLT.

SONNET

A ROSE as fair as ever saw the North,
Grew in a little garden all alone ;
A sweeter flower did Nature ne'er put forth,
Nor fairer garden yet was never known :
The maidens danc'd about it morn and noon,
And learned bards of it their ditties made ;

ROSES OF THE TWILIGHT

The nimble fairies by the pale-faced moon
Water'd the root and kiss'd her pretty shade.
But well-a-day the gardener careless grew ;
The maids and fairies both were kept away,
And in a drought the caterpillars threw
Themselves upon the bud and every spray.
    God shield the stock ! if heaven send no supplies,
    The fairest blossom of the garden dies.

WILLIAM BROWNE.

THE DESERTED GARDEN

I MIND me in the days departed,
How often underneath the sun
With childish bounds I used to run
    To a garden long deserted.

The beds and walks were vanished quite ;
And wheresoe'er had struck the spade,
The greenest grasses Nature laid,
    To sanctify her right.

I called the place my wilderness,
For no one entered there but I ;
The sheep looked in, the grass to espy,
    And passed it ne'ertheless.

The trees were interwoven wild,
And spread their boughs enough about
To keep both sheep and shepherd out,
    But not a happy child.

Adventurous joy it was for me!
I crept beneath the boughs, and found
A circle smooth of mossy ground
　　Beneath a poplar tree.

Old garden rose-trees hedged it in,
Bedropt with roses waxen-white,
Well satisfied with dew and light
　　And careless to be seen.

Long years ago it might befall,
When all the garden flowers were trim,
The grave old gardener prided him
　　On these the most of all.

Some lady, stately overmuch,
Here moving with a silken noise,
Has blushed beside them at the voice
　　That likened her to such.

And these, to make a diadem,
She often may have plucked and twined,
Half smiling as it came to mind
　　That few would look at *them*.

Oh, little thought that lady proud,
A child would watch her fair white rose,
When buried lay her whiter brows,
　　And silk was changed for shroud!—

Nor thought that gardener (full of scorns
For men unlearned and simple phrase),
A child would bring it all its praise
　　By creeping through the thorns!

'MOORLAND'

To me upon my low moss seat,
Though never a dream the roses sent
Of science or love's compliment,
   I ween they smelt as sweet.

It did not move my grief to see
The trace of human step departed :
Because the garden was deserted,
   The blither place for me !

Friends, blame me not ! a narrow ken
Has childhood 'twixt the sun and sward :
We draw the moral afterward—
   We feel the gladness then.

And gladdest hours for me did glide
In silence at the rose-tree wall ;
A thrush made gladness musical
   Upon the other side.

Nor he nor I did e'er incline
To peck or pluck the blossoms white ;
How should I know but roses might
   Lead lives as glad as mine ?

To make my hermit home complete,
I brought clear water from the spring
Praised in its own low murmuring,—
   And cresses glossy wet.

And so, I thought, my likeness grew
(Without the melancholy tale)
To ' gentle hermit of the dale,'
   And Angelina too.

For oft I read within my nook
Such minstrel stories ; till the breeze
Made sounds poetic in the trees,—
   And then I shut the book.

If I shut this wherein I write
I hear no more the wind athwart
Those trees,—nor feel that childish heart
   Delighting in delight.

My childhood from my life is parted,
My footstep from the moss which drew
Its fairy circle round : anew
   The garden is deserted.

Another thrush may there rehearse
The madrigals which sweetest are ;
No more for me !—myself afar
   Do sing a sadder verse.

Ah me, ah me ! when erst I lay
In that child's-nest so greenly wrought,
I laughed unto myself and thought
   ' The time will pass away.'

And still I laughed, and did not fear
But that, whene'er was past away
The childish time, some happier play
   My womanhood would cheer.

I knew the time would pass away,
And yet, beside the rose-tree wall,
Dear God, how seldom, if at all,
   Did I look up to pray !

The time is past ;—and now that grows
The cypress high among the trees,
And I behold white sepulchres
    As well as the white rose,—

When graver, meeker thoughts are given,
And I have learnt to lift my face,
Reminded how earth's greenest place
    The colour draws from heaven,—

It something saith for earthly pain,
But more for Heavenly promise free,
That I who was, would shrink to be
    That happy child again.

                E. B. BROWNING.

IN YON GARDEN

IN yon garden fine and gay,
Picking lilies a' the day,
Gathering flowers o' ilka hue,
I wistna then what love could do.

Where love is planted there it grows ;
It buds and blooms like any rose ;
It has a sweet and pleasant smell ;
No flower on earth can it excel.

I put my hand into the bush,
    And thought the sweetest rose to find ;
But pricked my finger to the bone,
    And left the sweetest rose behind.

                ANON.

OPHELIA

THERE runs a crisscross pattern of small leaves
Espalier, in a fading summer air,
And there Ophelia walks, an azure flower,
Whom wind, and snowflakes, and the sudden rain
Of love's wild skies have purified to heav'n.
There is a beauty past all weeping now
In that sweet crooked mouth, that vacant smile ;
Only a lonely grey in those mad eyes,
Which never on earth shall learn their loneliness.
And when 'mid startled birds she sings lament,
Mocking in hope the long voice of the stream,
It seems her heart's lute hath a broken string.
Ivy she hath, that to old ruin clings ;
And rosemary, that sees remembrance fade ;
And pansies, deeper than the gloom of dreams ;
But ah ! if utterable, would this earth
Remain the base, unreal thing it is ?
Better be out of sight of peering eyes ;
Out—out of hearing of all useless words,
Spoken of tedious tongues in heedless ears !
And lest, at last, the world should learn heart-secrets ;
Lest that sweet wolf from some dim thicket steal ;
Better the glassy horror of the stream !

WALTER DE LA MARE.

THE GARDEN OF LOVE

I WENT to the Garden of Love,
And saw what I never had seen :
A chapel was built in the midst,
Where I used to play on the green.

And the gates of this Chapel were shut,
And ' Thou shalt not ' writ over the door ;
So I turn'd to the Garden of Love
That so many sweet flowers bore ;

And I saw it was filled with graves,
And tombstones where flowers should be ;
And priests in black gowns were walking their rounds,
And binding with briars my joys and desires.

BLAKE.

MY LOVE BUILT ME A BONNIE
BOWER

MY love built me a bonnie bower,
And clad it a' wi' lily flower ;
A brawer bower ye ne'er did see,
Than my true lover built for me.

There cam a man at midday hour,
He heard my song and he saw my bower,
And he brocht armed men that nicht
And brak my bower and slew my knicht.

He slew my knicht, to me sae dear,
And burnt my bower, and drave my gear ;
My servants a' for life did flee,
And left me in extremitie.

I sew'd his sheet and made my mane,
I watch'd his corpse, myself alane ;
I watch'd by nicht and I watch'd by day,
No living creature cam that way.

K

I bore his body on my back,
And whyles I went, and whyles I sat ;
I digg'd a grave and laid him in,
And happ'd him wi' the sod sae green.

But think na ye my heart was sair,
When I laid the moul' on his yellow hair ?
Oh, think na ye my heart was wae,
When I turn'd about awa' to gae ?

The man lives not I 'll love again,
Since that my comely knicht is slain ;
Wi' ae lock of his yellow hair
I 'll bind my heart for evermair.

ANON.

FINE FLOWERS IN THE VALLEY

SHE sat down below a thorn,
   Fine flowers in the valley ;
And there she has her sweet babe born,
   And the green leaves they grow rarely.

' Smile na sae sweet, my bonny babe,
An ye smile sae sweet, ye 'll smile me dead.'

She 's ta'en out her little penknife,
And twinned the sweet babe o' its life.

She 's howket a grave by the light o' the moon,
And there she 's buried her sweet babe in.

70

As she was going to the church,
She saw a sweet babe in the porch.

'O sweet babe, if thou wert mine,
I wad cleed thee in silk and sabelline.'

'O mother mine, when I was thine,
You didna prove to me sae kind.

'But now I'm in the heavens hie,
  Fine flowers in the valley;
And ye have the pains o' hell to dree,
  And the green leaves they grow rarely.'

ANON.

A LATE WALK

WHEN I go up through the mowing field,
  The headless aftermath,
Smooth-laid like thatch with the heavy dew,
  Half closes the garden path.

And when I come to the garden ground,
  The whirr of sober birds
Up from the tangle of withered weeds
  Is sadder than any words.

A tree beside the wall stands bare,
  But a leaf that lingered brown,
Disturbed, no doubt, by my thought,
  Comes softly rattling down.

I end not far from my going forth
  By picking the faded blue
Of the last remaining aster flower
  To carry again to you.

ROBERT FROST.

THE END OF SUMMER

THE Dandelion sails away,—
  Some other port for him next spring;
Since they have seen the harvest home,
  Sweet birds have little more to sing.

Since from her side the corn is ta'en,
  The Poppy thought to win some praise;
But birds sang ne'er a welcome note,
  So she blushed scarlet all her days.

The children strip the blackberry bush,
  And search the hedge for bitter sloe;
They bite the sloes, now sweet as plums—
  After Jack Frost has bit them so.

'Twas this Jack Frost, one week ago,
  Made watch-dogs whine with fear and cold;
But all he did was make fruits smell,
  And make their coats to shine like gold.

No scattering force is in the wind,
  Though strong to shake the leaf from stem;
The leaves get in the rill's sweet throat,
  His voice is scarcely heard through them.

72

The darkest woods let in the light,
  And thin and frail are looking now;
And yet their weight is more than June's,
  Since nuts bend down each hazel bough.

WILLIAM H. DAVIES.

THE ARBOUR

O THE tap-room in the Winter
  When the ground is white with snow,
But the arbour in the Summer
  When the honeysuckles blow!
So, landlord, ice the cider,
  And put rose-leaves in the beer;
And we 'll drink with any fellow
  Who will pay his footing here!

O a nightingale is singing
  In the lilac on the lawn,
And we 'll join him in his chorus
  Till the day begins to dawn!
So, landlord, ice the cider,
  And put rose-leaves in the beer;
And we 'll drink with any fellow
  Who will pay his footing here!

O the moon lights up the lilies
  Through the blossoms on the lime;
But the rising sun is better
  For a clock for closing time!
So, landlord, ice the cider,
  And put rose-leaves in the beer;
And we 'll drink with any fellow
  Who will pay his footing here!

CHARLES DALMON.

ANOTHER SPRING

IF I might see another Spring
   I 'd not plant summer flowers and wait :
I 'd have my crocuses at once,
My leafless pink mezereons,
     My chill-veined snowdrops, choicer yet
     My white or azure violet,
Leaf-nested primrose ; anything
     To blow at once not late.

If I might see another Spring
   I 'd listen to the daylight birds
That build their nests and pair and sing,
Nor wait for mateless nightingale ;
     I 'd listen to the lusty herds,
     The ewes with lambs as white as snow,
I 'd find out music in the hail
     And all the winds that blow.

If I might see another Spring—
   Oh stinging comment on my past
That all my past results in ' If '—
   If I might see another Spring
I 'd laugh to-day, to-day is brief ;
I would not wait for anything :
     I 'd use to-day that cannot last,
     Be glad to-day and sing.

CHRISTINA ROSSETTI.

HONEYSUCKLE

THE CRAB AND MAPLE TREES
IN MILFIELD

THE cheerefull byrde that skips from tree to tree,
By skilfull choyse doth roust and rest at night :
Although by wing and will he may go free,
Yet there he pearkes, where most he takes delight.
As Thrush in thorne, and golden Finch in Fearne,
Great byrds in groves, the smale in bushie hedge :
The Larke alowe, in loftie tree the Hearne,
And some in Fenne, doe shrowde themselves in
    sedge.
So some men bost in Bayes, whose branch they
    beare,
Some Hawthorne hold, as chiefe of their delight :
Some wofull wightes, the wrethed Willows weare,
Some Roses reach, and some the Lyllies white.
Some Plane tree praise, as great Darius sonne,
Whose oft recourse thereto doth well expresse,
That vertues rise therin this Prince had wonne,
To like the same above the rest I gesse.
The Oliander eke, whose Roselike floure,
Faire Polixene so passing well did please :
Some lift aloft, and some the Pien pure,
Yet trees I know that farre surmounteth these.
Not for their daintie fruites, or odoures sweete,
Ne yet for sumptuous shewe that others yeelde :
But for the Ladies sakes, which there did meete,
I give them prayse as chiefest in the fielde.
O happy trees, O happy boughes, whose shade
Ishrouded hath such Noble vertuous wightes :
By whom you were, and are a Mirror made,
Who of your selves doe yeelde no great delightes.

O fertyle ground, in yeelding wise that lends
Such causes greate of Ladies perfite joyes,
O blissefull place so fit for faithfull friends,
In pleasures ryse, to rid them from anoyes.
What wonder may it be, to those shall heare,
In Maple hard, or crooked Crabbe tree sowre :
Such sugred talke, such jests, such joyfull cheare,
Such mylde affects, as if 'twere Cupids bowre ?
Now sith these Noble Nimphes ybreathed have,
Upon these plants, in uttering forth their minde :
If any seeke their secrecie to crave,
High Jove I pray these trees may shew their kinde.
Help Satyrs eke, you Gods that keepe the wood,
The poysoning breath of Boreas rough resist :
And thou whose sylver drops bedewes eche bud,
Refresh these trees with sweete Auroraes mist.
And Jove if thou in Milfeelde shew thy might,
Convert them soone, to fruites of more delight,
    That Maple may be Mulberie,
    And Crabbe tree eke a Medler be.

THOMAS HOWELL

UPON THE PRIORY GROVE

HIS USUAL RETIREMENT

HAIL, sacred shades ! cool leafy house !
Chaste treasurer of all my vows
And wealth ! on whose soft bosom laid
My love's fair steps I first betrayed :
Henceforth no melancholy flight,
No sad wing, or hoarse bird of Night,
Disturb this air, no fatal throat

Of raven, or owl, awake the note
Of our laid echo, no voice dwell
Within these leaves but Philomel.
The poisonous ivy here no more
Her false twists on the oak shall score ;
Only the woodbine here may twine,
As th' emblem of her love, and mine ;
The amorous sun shall here convey
His best beams in thy shade to play ;
The active air, the gentlest showers
Shall from his wings rain on thy flowers ;
And the moon from her dewy locks,
Shall deck thee with her brightest drops :
Whatever can a fancy move,
Or feed the eye : be on this grove.
    And when, at last, the winds and tears
Of Heaven, with the consuming years,
Shall these green curls bring to decay,
And clothe thee in an aged grey :—
If aught a lover can foresee :
Or if we poets prophets be—
From hence transplanted, thou shalt stand
A fresh grove in th' Elysian land ;
Where—most blest pair !—as here on Earth
Thou first didst eye our growth, and birth ;
So there again, thou 'lt see us move
In our first innocence and love ;
And in thy shades, as now, so then,
We 'll kiss, and smile, and walk again.

HENRY VAUGHAN.

THE ATTENDANT SPIRIT IN 'COMUS' EPILOGUISES

TO the ocean now I fly,
And those happy climes that lie
Where day never shuts his eye,
Up in the broad fields of the sky.
There I suck the liquid air,
All amidst the gardens fair
Of Hesperus, and his daughters three
That sing about the golden tree.
Along the crisped shades and bowers
Revels the spruce and jocund Spring :
The Graces and the rosy-bosomed Hours
Thither all their bounties bring.
There eternal Summer dwells ;
And west winds with musky wing
About the cedarn alleys fling
Nard, and cassia's balmy smells.
Iris there with humid bow
Waters the odorous banks, that blow
Flowers of more mingled hue
Than her purfled scarf can shew,
And drenches with Elysian dew
(List, mortals, if your ears be true)
Beds of hyacinth and roses,
Where young Adonis oft reposes,
Waxing well of his deep wound,
In slumber soft, and on the ground
Sadly sits the Assyrian queen.
But far above, in spangled sheen,
Celestial Cupid, her famed son, advanced
Holds his dear Psyche, sweet entranced

GRASS OF PARNASSUS

After her wandering labours long,
Till free consent the gods among
Make her his eternal bride ;
And from her fair unspotted side
Two blissful twins are to be born,
Youth and Joy ; so Jove hath sworn.
   But now my task is smoothly done,
I can fly, or I can run
Quickly to the green earth's end,
Where the bowed welkin slow doth bend ;
And from thence can soar as soon
To the corners of the moon.
   Mortals that would follow me,
Love Virtue ; she alone is free.
She can teach ye how to climb
Higher than the sphery chime ;
Or, if Virtue feeble were,
Heaven itself would stoop to her.

MILTON.

SONG

A SPIRIT haunts the year's last hours
Dwelling amid these yellowing bowers :
      To himself he talks ;
For at eventide, listening earnestly,
At his work you may hear him sob and sigh
      In the walks ;
      Earthward he boweth the heavy stalks
Of the mouldering flowers :
      Heavily hangs the broad sunflower
         Over its grave i' the earth so chilly ;
      Heavily hangs the hollyhock,
         Heavily hangs the tiger-lily.

79

The air is damp, and hush'd, and close,
As a sick man's room when he taketh repose
    An hour before death ;
My very heart faints and my whole soul grieves
At the moist rich smell of the rotting leaves,
    And the breath
    Of the fading edges of box beneath,
And the year's last rose.
    Heavily hangs the broad sunflower
      Over its grave i' the earth so chilly ;
    Heavily hangs the hollyhock,
      Heavily hangs the tiger-lily.

TENNYSON.

CANDLEMAS EVE

DOWN with the rosemary and bays,
    Down with the mistletoe ;
Instead of holly, now upraise
    The greener box, for show.

The holly hitherto did sway ;
    Let box now domineer
Until the dancing Easter Day
    Or Easter's eve appear.

Then youthful box, which now hath grace
    Your houses to renew,
Grown old, surrender must his place
    Unto the crispèd yew.

OCTOBER ROSES

.

When yew is out, then birch comes in,
   And many flowers beside,
Both of a fresh and fragrant kin,
   To honour Whitsuntide.

Green rushes then, and sweetest bents,
   With cooler oaken boughs,
Come in for comely ornaments,
   To re-adorn the house.
Thus times do shift, each thing his turn does hold ;
New things succeed, as former things grow old.

HERRICK.

EAGER SPRING

WHIRL, snow, on the blackbird's chatter ;
You will not hinder his song to come.
East wind, sleepless, you cannot scatter
Quince-bud, almond-bud,
Little grape-hyacinth's
Clustering brood,
Nor unfurl the tips of the plum.
No half-born stalk of a lily stops ;
There is sap in the storm-torn bush ;
And, ruffled by gusts in a snow-blurred copse,
' Pity to wait ' sings a thrush.

Love, there are few Springs left for us ;
They go, and the count of them as they go
Makes surer the count that is left for us.
More than the east wind, more than the snow,

81

I would put back these hours that bring
Buds and bees and are lost ;
I would hold the night and the frost,
To save for us one more Spring.

GORDON BOTTOMLEY.

APRIL   MORNING